*Holding
Company*

Also by Major Jackson

Hoops
Leaving Saturn

Holding
Company

Major Jackson

W. W. Norton & Company
New York · London

Excerpt from "T. S. Eliot" from *Collected Poems* by Robert Lowell.
Copyright © 2003 by Harriet Lowell and Sheridan Lowell. Reprinted by
permission of Farrar, Straus and Giroux, LLC.

Excerpt from "Plan of Future Works" from *Poems* by Pier Paolo Pasolini,
translated by Norman MacAfee. Translation copyright © 1982 by
Norman MacAfee. Reprinted by permission of Farrar, Straus and
Giroux, LLC.

For information about permission to reproduce selections from this book,
write to Permissions, W. W. Norton & Company, Inc.,
500 Fifth Avenue, New York, NY 10110

For information about special discounts for bulk purchases, please contact
W. W. Norton Special Sales at specialsales@wwnorton.com or
800-233-4830

Manufacturing by Courier Westford
Book design by Charlotte Staub
Production manager: Anna Oler

Library of Congress Cataloging-in-Publication Data

Jackson, Major, 1968–
Holding company / Major Jackson. — 1st ed.
p. cm.
ISBN 978-0-393-07080-4 (hardcover)
I. Title.
PS3610.A354H65 2010
811'.6—dc22

                                    2010017728

W. W. Norton & Company, Inc.
500 Fifth Avenue, New York, N.Y. 10110
www.wwnorton.com

W. W. Norton & Company Ltd.
Castle House, 75/76 Wells Street, London W1T 3QT

1 2 3 4 5 6 7 8 9 0

For

James Welden Romare Jackson

and

in memory of
my mother

Gloria Ann Matthews

Contents

Your Hourglass & No One Else to Blame

Picket Monsters 3
Creationism 4
Going to Meet the Man 5
White Power 6
Mondes en Collision 7
Migration 8
After Riefenstahl 9
Roof of the World 10
Discrete Intelligence 11
Greek Revival 12
Said the Translator 13
Jane Says 14
Lost Lake 15
I Had the Craziest Dream 16
Life During Wartime 17
Dynagroove 18
Hysteresis 19
Exquisite Minutes 20
Tremble 21
You, who carry daylight on your face 22

Unteachable Rain

New Sphere of Influence 25

Towers 26

Anthrodrome 27

Poem Beginning with a Line by Dante Rossetti 28

Heaven Goes Online 29

Thinking of Lucretius 30

Aubade 31

Speaking East Coast 32

The Nature of Affairs 33

At the Club 34

Strangers Are Not Strangers 35

On Removing the Wedding Band 36

Superfluities 37

Headfirst 38

The Chase 39

How You Love 40

Club Revival 41

Quaff 42

Bedraggled 43

More Feeling 44

Caressing the Ruins

Jewel-Tongued 47

Manna 48

Bereft 49

Shortbus 50

Hookups 51

Breakups 52

Early Spring 53

Roadblocks 54

Digging Holes 55

Delicious. I love you. Goodbye. 56

The Door I Open 57

Therapy 58

Far Out West 59

When you go away 60

Designer Kisses 61

Fever 62

Observe His Face 63

Homecoming 64

Lorca in Eden 65

Myth 66

An Empire of Hand-Holding & Park Benches

Autumn Landscape 69

My Awe Is a Weakness 70

Headstones 71

Immanence 72

Recondite 73

Prayer 74

On the Manner of Addressing Shadows 75

Overwrought Power Ballad 76

Narcissus 77

Lying 78

The Giant Swing Ending in a Split 79

Treat the Flame 80
Periplum 81
My Face in the ATM Screen 82
Maithuna 83
Here the Sea 84
Brash and Ambitious 85
Leave It All Up to Me 86
Zucchini 87
Forecast 88

Notes 89
About the Author 93

Acknowledgments

Grateful acknowledgment is made to editors of the following publications, anthologies, and Web sites in which some of these poems originally appeared: *AGNI*, *The American Poetry Review*, *Ashville Poetry Review*, *Black Nature: Four Centuries of African American Nature Poetry*, *The Cortland Review*, *Ecotone*, failbetter.com, *Fence*, *From the Fishouse: An Anthology of Poems that Sing, Rhyme, Resound, Syncopate, Alliterate, and Just Plain Sound Great*, *Luna: A Journal of Poetry and Translation*, *Harvard Review*, *jubilat*, *Memorius 10*, *New Orleans Review*, *Northwest Review*, *The Paris Review*, *Ploughshares*, *A Public Space*, *Sugar House Review*, *Quarterly West*, *The Queen City Review*, *Tuesday Journal*, and *Zoland Poetry 3*.

It is a pleasure to thank the Radcliffe Institute for Advanced Study at Harvard University and the Sidney Harman Writer-in-Residence Program at Baruch College for time and resources to complete this manuscript. I thank my colleagues at the University of Vermont, New York University, and Bennington Writing Seminars for inspiration.

I am also ever grateful for dear compatriots, friends, and family who support and hold dear my company. Most of all, I'd like to thank my angel on earth Vicki Zubovic for her never-ending patience, discerning eye, intelligence, love, and support.

. . . one muse, one music, had one the luck—
  lost in the dark night of the brilliant talkers.

—Robert Lowell, on T. S. Eliot

Then

once those expressionistic candles have been lit
at the altars of sex, I'll return to religion.
.

.

.

and finally I'll reveal my true passion:

Which is life raging [or unwilling] [or dying]
—and thus, again poetry:
neither the sign nor the existing thing matters.

—Pier Paolo Pasolini,
Plan of Future Works

Holding
Company

Your Hourglass &
No One Else to Blame

Picket Monsters

For I was born, too, in the stunted winter of History.
For I, too, desired the Lion's mouth split
& the world that is not ours, and the wounded children
set free to their turnstiles of wonder. I, too, have
blinked speechless at the valleys of corpses, wished
Scriabin's "Black Mass" in the Executioner's ear,
Ellington in the Interrogation Room.
I now seek gardens where bodies have their will,
where the self is a compass point given to the lost.
Let me call your name; the ground here is soft & broken.

Creationism

I gave the bathtub purity and honor, and the sky
noctilucent clouds, and the kingfisher his implacable
devotees. I gave salt & pepper the table, and the fist
its wish for bloom, and the net, knotholes of emptiness.
I gave the loaf its slope of integrity, the countertop
belief in the horizon, and mud its defeated boots.
I gave morning triumphant songs which consume my pen,
and death its grief which is like a midsummer thunderclap.
But I did not give her my tomblike woe though it trembled
from my white bones and shook the walls of our home.

Going to Meet the Man

As if one day, a grand gesture of the mind, an expired
subscription to silence, a decision raw as a concert
of habaneros on the lips, a renewal to decency like a trash
can smashing a storefront or shattering the glass face
of a time clock: where once a man forced to the ground,
a woman spread-eagled against a wall, where a blast into
the back of an unarmed teen: finally, a decisive spark,
the engine of action, a civilian standoff: on one side,
a barricade of shields, helmets, batons, and pepper spray:
on the other, a cocktail of fire, all that is just and good.

White Power

As it happened, I was twirling a cauliflower floret,
lost in Lewis's wardrobe of pallid trees,
considering my country's longing for homogenized milk
& bags of tube socks from Walmart,
which felt cancerous. What came to me like a surprise
snowfall in the soft evening of a snow globe,
one has to pinch salt and sprinkle in the palm,
repeatedly, especially when the temperature in mother's
 trailer
has begun to drop. In this way, after your Constitution fades,
you've your own hourglass and no one else to blame.

Mondes en Collision

To the question of history's tectonic drift,
Immanuel Velikovsky removed his glasses & pinched
his temples before a silent throng at the Royal
Hypnagogic Society in Edmonton. Through a window,
coppiced trees blurred. An orange-headed thrush
fleetingly invaded his sight. Someone coughed.
Despair fell into despair, building its music. The abrupt clash
of meaning was like the laughter of running children.
He saw the microphone's convexed portals as one
of many recognizable texts out of our celestial holes.

Migration

That summer, municipality was on everyone's lips,
even the earth eaters who put the pastor in pastoral.
Truth is my zeal for chicory waned, and my chest was damp.
I shivered by a flagpole, knowing betrayal
was coming my way. Just the same, I believed like a guitar
      string
believes in distance and addressed each bright star *Lord*
of My Feet. A country of overnight deputies, everyone had a
      knot
to endeavor. I read oaks and poplars for signs: charred
      branches,
tobacco leaves strung up to die, swamp soil in my soul. Ever
      trace
the outline of a phantom mob, even if you were late
      arriving?

After Riefenstahl

The screen's fabrications remain. A film
shot never fails, sailing through the century
like a black V at the hour of moaning.
I premiere these pontifical birds: villagers march
and raise their arms, *Marschlieder*. Thus I am
your sweet messenger glittering more than first stars,
a harvest of light concealing your nicks and little deaths.
My comrade, my camera, my power, my fury,
my triumph, my will: do you not also,
my love, flicker in a cathedral of terror?

Roof of the World

I live on the roof of the world among the aerial
simulacra of Things, among the faded: old tennis shoes,
vanished baseballs, heartbreak gritted with dirt. My mind
flickers like lightning in a cloud. I'm networked
beholding electric wires and church spires.
I lean forward and peer at the suffering below—
Sartre said: man is condemned to be free.
I believe in the dead who claim to believe in me—
says, too, the missing and forgotten. Day darkens
on. I hear our prayers rising. I sing to you, now.

Discrete Intelligence

Hotels take up where bedrooms leave off.
Crucifixes find their way above senate bills.
A one-sided temper precedes a major pact.
Belowstairs cowers beneath abovestairs.
Meanwhile ghettos torment our nightsheets.
Presidential invasion escalates insurgencies.
A mistress puts on gloves and holds her breath.
Then the follow-up, we're adamant about dreamless
days, the all-out assault on ambiguity,
the tee-off, the golf swing, the far-look away.

Greek Revival

Of that unhurried blink of eyelids I glimpsed, all pixilated
and grains, belonging to a woman dying, on screen
her life winding down, yet one last cinematic glance
in the prime like a loose smile filling the frame
over a shoulder, I say so much lateral interpolations
    fasten us
to that sequence of flowers as sped-up funerals. I thought
this stepping up in the Garden District to a streetcar.
The avenue *has* rituals: the curved horizon of Southern
mansions, and the gripping anguish of oak branches
    reaching
through half-opened windows like desperate fingers.

Said the Translator

Plato would be easier, said the translator, and thus began
the factory tour. One had to understand the language
of AstroTurf dotted with cannons or the nonalcoholic joy
subway-watching women two-finger designer eyewear
firmly up the bridge, all that rollicking uncertainty
like a root beer. Who cares about splitting hairs
when what's at stake is merely the history of robes?
The clock read 12:13, exactly when no seven were alike,
yet, give him a pencil and the knotholes of other mouths
make a soft hollow noise. All he knows is what he thinks.

Jane Says

I only know they want me, prone to stupefaction
at the ambivalence of men. The house is sleeping,
but she's flipping through American Spirits,
the canned laughter of heroin nights. Her oneiric
fades: prairie grass bending away, barnyard decay,
red-checkered tableware, summer running liquid
air, languorous lift of an American flag, her grandparents
waving, her faded duffle bag, the Irish setter
spiraling in circles. A patrol car paints more tattoos,
and out of silence, they move, too, like green vines.

Lost Lake

A soggy brightness at the northernmost ridge
of the Tahkenitch, even nearing dusk and not
a Domino's for miles. I said holy at a coniferous wall
of western hemlock overhead and red cedar
which rose up from the foot of that coastal creek
bearing its image and all around. I had not known
I'd come as a witness. The great Pacific rolled in
news from distant shores beyond a stretch of dune
trails behind us. White-winged gulls shrieked
and flapped at our misery frothing in waves.

I Had the Craziest Dream

Never on Sunday she said and brandished
an oval locket of hairs from each
of her lovers. I looked over my shoulders.
We sat munching on puffs of dried hydrangea
that no surprise tasted of cotton candy.
Far off on the sea, on a floating bench,
my mother excitedly talked up the president.
I questioned his killing clothes, and knew it all perishable
at any moment. The pictures were hanging themselves.
Along our coastline. *Best* she said *to hammer in the*
 morning.

Life During Wartime

But the daydream collapses and time returns us
to corners where young boys expire
like comets at the suburbs of your thalamus.
Gunshots weaken the houses; hope vanishes
like old cell phones. Blood darkens a stoop;
the mouth is disagreeable. But then, one afternoon,
a sunshower baptizes shadows on a street. The steaming
scent of wet sidewalks swells your insides
and somewhere not far from here a young girl grabs
the hand of a boy and runs over the rubble.

Dynagroove

Our social clock had gone berserk but those
groovy Eames and collectible lamps licensed
us to practice a kind of savage civility. Our vice
wasn't noble or the avalanche of cocktails
with serene names suggestive of spy movies
or the imprudent idea of going further in snow.
We secretly wished for living rooms with such large
cushions. We might have survived it all, especially
the piñata beatings of effigies in foreign deserts we had
no idea existed. Even the bongos promised Heaven.

Hysteresis

The chancellor leaning in the chaise
thought, "In the old days we liked to eat well."
The wood-paneled room conjured greater wistfulness
swell enough for him to finger an inside pocket
for a phantom cigar which he lit to an Edwardian blaze,
surprised to find his mind more than a night machine
sputtering pearls. He missed the old chaps at the club,
a fit citizenry if ever there were one. All is changed:
everywhere patterns in the dark-grain
swirling their exotic typhoons.

Exquisite Minutes

When we are separated on two train platforms,
the other's antithesis for the 7:20 Express,
think of it as some angel-liberating moment
sans the putrid swoosh of subway air.
The radio struggles to neaten its long wave ban.
Its susceptibility to seraphic interference
reveals the white fractures of our bare intelligence.
Yet some of us arrive capable of reading
the clanks of tracks, lights in a tunnel,
the arrival of birds in underground channels.

Tremble

My neighbor is velvety and kicks serious game.
So sweet garlic refuses to hang tight
in his mouth. He pulls women to his wide chest
each time as if he's won the Lotto. He rocks
them gently and gentler. My neighbor
is a master spooner. He knows not of desire, but only
the rules of engagement. He says, *I miss*
having Skype on all night so I can listen
to your breathing. He floats in his museum,
of gams, drifting from frame to frame.

You, who carry daylight on your face

You, who carry daylight on your face
the best of us all, the sky is lust,
and stills my zippered spine. Observe my envy
of the sea where you wade, its surface
like an afternoon of swordplay.
You shun the lips of infants disguised as men.
Young girls cherish the mirrors where you
quickly collect yourself. The neighbors
know your comings and goings, but the syntax
of your smiles is revealed only to little children.

Unteachable Rain

New Sphere of Influence

This is the year I'll contemplate the fire-fangled sky
over the isle of Pag, authored by my lover's eyes.
A crimson rambler uncurls its petals, and I am whistling
a dusty concerto, "Hope with Roadside Wildflowers."
I want to unfurl in the sodden fields of her daydreams.
Who wants immortality if she must die?
Once I thought stars were everlasting, only dying
behind a cerulean curtain, cloudy rains at dawn.
My lover's lips are twin geniuses. I've trashed the movie stubs
of my past. I've front row seats to her mumbling sleep.

Towers

I could give your palace more glass shine,
facing eastward every year without knowing.
And no, it's not convincing waking in fog and rain,
steel and stone soaring above the living. After many
springs, streets accrue their grief, and the people
are nameless. I broadcast my hunger,
heartwood beneath skin radiant as coronas—
what's there: son of tenderness, son of disasters.
When the lonely swirl nights, I run toward them,
a concentric eyewall, my indestructible hunger.

Anthrodrome

She was light as a shadow. I wanted
to know her better than the rest
before me. I promised her neither miracles
or hallucinations and mixtaped all
my ecstasies starting first with Sembène.
Out of my mouth came the wind
of my birth. Out of my hands poured unteachable
rain. Seeing nothing but inappropriate sentinels,
products of major antagonisms from a far-off century,
we said *Good-bye* to our once born emptiness.

Poem Beginning with a Line
by Dante Rossetti

Because dear God the flesh thou madest smooth
seems moments ago molded, who had
stared before on her, sheen of new
limbs, wet taking shape, lifewind blown
to penetrate pores, rainwater runneling
in soft torrents? Those smatterings of blackbirds
and finches, those nearby scrubby trees, her loofah:
even these seem to possess the painter's
stout gaze, usurping human's very matter,
a haloed canvas splashed with our suffering.

Heaven Goes Online

When the sidewalk's eyes were weeping
when snowflakes burst from the pillows
as the mayor talked from the bottlecaps of his ears
& the old women dusted off their beauty marks
when the graffiti artist's hand became a saffron scarf
when the breeze flashed its grilled teeth
& the sun torched the forest to a moon
when sad Amelia pierced the clouds in her veins
when my lips gathered at the beaches of your lips
& my tongue at the on-ramp of your spine

Thinking of Lucretius

I follow her to the floor of a canvas,
to bonfires at daybreak, to highways of scenic
strangeness, to calla lilies alive in courtyards of pain,
past fathers marching in mud, silence, and rain,
to battlefields and fissures in earth, beyond
baroque façades and that rapt spell of widening voices
arguing with the sea. Then, and only then, do our shadows
commence their deep communion, and a summer evening
of stars yawns its bare shimmering. We stare down
the arson in us with a ceiling fan turning above.

Aubade

Beyond the limits of myself, there is you, a wind-wave
of fading light on a square of cottage pane,
a final mix of golden prairie in my mind.
I am the impoverished heir of blackened gum quarters,
your crosswalk & roofline of foul pigeons. Dear Sibilant
    Stir & Kick:
see that tall grass on the ceiling, that burst of dusted corn,
that sky advancing its phalanx of irritable clouds?
I rest my hand on your thigh beneath its silk chemise,
so like a mid-surge surf of turquoise sky stilled.
Whichever way your shoulder moves, there's joy.

Speaking East Coast

As if hypnotized by the illicit pleasure
of her barely touching hand on his cheek
and her eyes pressed to his mouth and her lips
fixed in paradise, the taxi driver, peering in his
rear-view and long arrived at the hotel with its revolving
doors they'll not use, for a doorman will open with
great somberness so they can disappear, anxious
to ascend and commence their marathon to purity,
gazes back to his farebox, its bright numbers
now thundering louder than ever before.

The Nature of Affairs

Each time, as if we were born blinking
to ourselves, pushing into an expectant world—
the shocking smell of chlorine at the edge,
yet, an accountable, country club sweetness, too,
that reigns for awhile, sensuous luxury
that makes early morning kisses, normally brocaded
and fetid, like little sips of martinis. Lost on the outskirts
of town, and in what surrounds us—dark abyss out
of which we drive headlights through the ghoulish air.

At the Club

Just then, I saw her inhabiting me and inhabiting me
from other mornings of her own molding.
I moved like an island bequeathed to the forlorn.
The way light splashed across her nose
said she bore no razors in her night cream but
I had not the yoga to pour myself into one ocean
and lacked courage to unzip the skin of prisons
prized by the scarred and those who know
only how to breathe with their back to the horizon,
a vainglorious solo. She gave her license away in the dark.

Strangers Are Not Strangers

Winter's early evening, and I sculpt moonlit clouds
over our shoulders. Our bodies fall. The lamps
have their flickering. I've said a hundred prayers
to her knees, and now, I'm at work beating a drum for
our future, making ceremony of my dark hands.
Outside, thick skeins of black branches sway woozily.
I'm thinking of vineyards in Sardegna, thornbushes,
wood-scented apples, charms beneath fingernails.
What color's that cry trickling from her mouth?
In a sacred grove, we leave melodies on each other's skin.

On Removing the Wedding Band

As though undreaming the mountain
from the sea or tweezering hands from
a watch, a quick-fix change of regimes:
a democracy lost to a monarchy, an empty sudden
village, and elsewhere the wedding party lining up
like a lost tribe of refugees. As though a reverse
whisper of vows into a pageant of elegant ears
when the heat in the O cooled its "till death do us"
and the storm inside seething below
the flowers, gowns, and cake, its own Institution.

Superfluities

This downpour of bad reasoning, this age-old swarm,
this buzzing about town, this kick and stomp
through gardens, this snag on the way to the mall,
this heap and toss of fabric and strewn shoes, this tangled
beauty, this I came here not knowing, here
to be torched, this fumbling ecstasy, this ecstasy of fumbling,
this spray of lips and fingers, this scrape of bone, this raid
of private grounds, this heaving and rocking, this scream
and push, this sightless hunger, this tattered perishing,
this rhythmic teeth knocking, this unbearable
music, this motionless grip, grimace, and groan.

Headfirst

Elsewhere, fluids seeped in a coffin. A miser
fueling his car gawked at a constellation.
Confederate flags fluttered in Georgia.
A plane dropped suddenly then rose above
crumpled clouds. Last night, your torso was
full fledged like an aria or Ellington's hands
slashing downward then his sudden lift from
a piano bench. I admit: my solo was tucked
away in the lavish & vast wardrobe of misery.
I only just now gathered your complaint.

The Chase

"What are you thinking?" she said. "Falling pheasants."
He said. "Please look at me." she said.
"I've seen too much." he said. "You're like a wet cave."
She said. "You're a feast of rhythms." he said.
"I want more than thunderbolts inside." she said.
"Wave after wave after wave." he said. "Your eyes
are stitching tighter." she said. "I am lost in a blizzard
of feathers." he said. "You are lost." she said.

How You Love

Like the injured laid down at the scene of an accident
before cars collide, like cloud striations over
Fairyland Loop, like a kid's carnival balloon
diminishing and lost to the great blue,
like bright jewels scattered in some secret cave, like two
scissor blades breaking apart, like after-party guacamole
with drips of salsa, like diamonds of light rotating over
an empty dance floor, like priests at night staring
in store windows at half-nude mannequins,
like dark earwax, like unscented candles, like Janus.

Club Revival

The way the mountains bled purple that
one blue dusk announced
what savory thrusts were being born
inside us. Blessed are our bodies in clubs
like camp meetings charged to holy filaments.
Bless our husky-frolicking hymns,
and our tumultuous strains come bearing
down. We arise and drop, arise
and sway. Twigs crackle beneath our soles,
and those white-gloved hands encircle.

Quaff

Notable the covert springs of anger trickling,
wending its way, and the road invigorating
below stands of sycamore, oaks. It was
a competition of playlists. I wanted the freest poem
in the world. So I complimented her brows
seemingly to lift in intimate flight like a Truffaut scene,
which was catnip to her ears. The shifting
illuminations cast lines on the ceiling. Glug, glug.
Those first nights came to us again. We pulled
onto the breakdown lane and drank deep.

Bedraggled

All afternoon, plunging deeper and deeper.
I deplete myself noiselessly. The closet mirror
debuts again its silent film of capsized ships.
She sees me. I see her. We wave our first world premiere.
Don't look for father here whose kamikaze smile,
for all you know, is more Samaritan than
an Adirondack above the sea. How wonder struck
I seem draping my ballerina completing
her soprano bellow, what one must feel
when light rises from everywhere.

More Feeling

How did I come to make a crisis of the body?
I could give your palace more glass shine,
undreaming the sea from the mountains.
Had I possessed the poise to possess
my faraway thirst for mornings. I'm glum.
Your sportive flesh in the empire of blab
is the latest guy running his trendy tongue
as if every evening your body beneath his snarl.
Over our shoulders, our bodies fall—the lamps.
For I was born, too, in the muted winter of History.

Caressing the Ruins

Jewel-Tongued

How did I come to make a crisis
of the body, my fingers evaporating inside?
The stillness of a lover's mouth
assaulted me. I never wearied of anecdotes
on the Commons, gesturing until I scattered
myself into a luminance, shining over a village
of women. Was I less human or more? I hear still
my breathing echoing off their pillows. So many
eyes like crushed flowers. Our fingers splayed
over a bed's edge. We were blown away.

Manna

As if every evening your body is a smile
mingling with the sea or the sky's last song
over the cenotaph of violets wilting in Eastham.
On the day of the crime, the afternoon was empty.
We were footnotes on the beach and came back the color
of pancakes. I was giving the Rosicrucians another chance,
knowing how hunger prevails long after we've turned
our backs on cruelty toward Faulkner and Seneca.
My gratitude was fragile, for I was kissing the thorns.
"To sea! To sea!" shouted the marvelous girls, "To sea!"

Bereft

Seemingly without consequence, we're all here,
a tribunal of insomniacs. I'm the one leaping
like a dolphin catching treats. The room smells
of sand-crusted seaweed. In a single evening, soft women
have moved like windblown clouds over my dark body.
Your wife is not at home but hosting this spell
of fine light slanting through poplars outside
a bedroom window. Language died the moment
desire disrobed and bodies made fine striations
of solar flares. And while you sleep, a mouse
sniffs its snout along a baseboard floor.

Shortbus

But then this oceanic floor of desirous,
dowered flesh, slick, seal-like, nosing up,
the long blue swim through dim corridors,
bodies cinematically remixed to a set of empty drums.
Lonely is the night, nature's enzyme—how many
water faces floating below like iridescent lilies
have risen up to meet yours? How many writhing,
night-blooming, dew-washed women? You're prostrate
in the casket of your shadow. The hidden banks
of groans, the splendid whispered sighs beckon.

Hookups

They never flee from me, hobnobbers
of the dark moon—of their own accord,
moths mistaking the bulb. Like a mob
they swarm to my room. Bored
I lead them to the firmanent of touch:
forage my blues, they say, as such,
cloud formations who graze horrors,
then release their internal weathers. Boom
boom in the dark regions. I wish I'd pulled
the covers over my head and were left alone.

Breakups

When girls cried after I declared it over, I grew
an erection. For this I feel shame, but not
self-annihilation. Each time I thought of Troy
who once, after I stepped in the neighborhood
punch block, sidewalk brass medallion inset
advertising concrete, punched my stomach.
And though bent over and gasping, Troy kept
pummeling and wouldn't let me out—a game we played
till we saw tears—then later bragged, but not before offering
his arm, shrouding me, trying to calm a friend.

Early Spring

Now she is going with the rain, like a blinking
stoplight, falling methodically. Nothing
in the world is knowing. Her ears burst,
a slow suicide of clouds coerced
to reincarnate. I promised her long similes
and the wintry teeth of my smiles.
With her I wanted to park my prayers
beneath a billboard. My eyewear is
empty, as are my armpits. The milk in
the refrigerator has soured.

Roadblocks

Given said variance, rather my side of the orchard,
is it merely about the hookup where I'm legislating
other pods in daisies, an enormous yellow grove
between the gurney and the exhilaration of Formica
in her eyes? One touch of my hand, the gavel lands,
and she's constellated. I wandered through a feverish
belief in teeth biting grass, in half-awake moans.
Across the city of night, breasts, waists, throats pure
as punctuated skies. I took Mr. Blue to cafés, spoke grief
to all the distingué faces, also too, in the fly business.

Digging Holes

Consider this effervescing body a topiary,
greeting visitors at the edge of a college town,
or rather, grief disguised as feigned joy
flitting in and out of rhododendron
and lilac bushes. What I mean: twilight
in the backyard, explaining the women
away as nothing more than gray drifts
of cloud. Consider those echoes of passion
that rippled toward the bleak snowfields of my days
as slips on the ice when the globe arced.

Delicious. I love you. Goodbye.

Then to get down in the dark on hands and knees
and hear the most professional of human tones
like the overvoice in a theme park that says
The ride is over. Please step down carefully.
And it ain't the least bit diacritical. Don't mind that line
of dried, wilting bouquets behind him. Open
his mouth, dead birds fall out. Saddest of all
macabre excuses. All artists, it's true, set
their sights on you, ruthless Picasso. Broken
hearts in the name of art.

The Door I Open

The door I open to who I am is not a garage
of reminisces or a book with you
as an elastic notion represented in between
stanzas, thus a hall of *Mona Lisas*. The door
I open is a self-song furnishing the mind's
mansion. I observe no rules and ruin the hours.
Plato knew the poem as a sword moonlighting
as a mirror which correctly angled caught a surfeit
of light and threatened to blind the Republic—
our rotoscopic freedom at the foothills.

Therapy

Ashes of fire in his mouth, rain sloshed in
his head. He felt caressed once like a skyline.
Day of warm sunlight drowsing languidly
which was the damp belly of his sorrow.
He thought of his mother's muted, joyous cries,
and slumped further, only now in memory, smoke
curled from his lovers' lips, bursts of ghost-snakes.
He ambled, retracing steps from The Convenience Store,
yet all he could see were industrial clouds, dreaming
of avenues that ran straight and clean.

Far Out West

We spoke Stalin and Amin to the point of tears,
a time when I thought cruelty explained
everything: which of us asked for directions?
We longed for the painted eyelids of dowagers in Macy's.
I coughed badly that month in stairwells.
Storm clouds passed over the curbs of my ribs.
I walked from gallery to gallery sampling various delicacies.
Canvasses of lemon tisane & I thought of you.
Oh, the allure of remorseful despots! & I thought of you.
I no longer want this weather on my breath.

When you go away

I stand by a water cooler. Its upside-down
despondency and crock match the purity
of my melancholy. Think of Akhmatova's white
stone in the well. That morning you were
dispassionate about Raskolnikov and Pecola,
and pointed to our fingers and their chain of bones
pulling into a trainyard of subway stops. *Evidence
of the end of freight,* you said. It was pre-spring.
The sadness of melting snow hit me like a film thrown
suddenly in daylight. So, torture the gods.

Designer Kisses

I'm glum about your sportive flesh in the empire of blab,
and the latest guy running his trendy tongue like a
    tantalizing surge
over your molars, how droll. Love by a graveyard *is*
    redundant,
but the skin is an obstacle course like Miami where we are
inescapably consigned: tourists keeping the views new.
What as yet we desire, our own fonts of adoration. By
    morning,
we're laid out like liquid timepieces, each other's exercise
    in perpetual
enchantment, for there is that beach in us that is
    untranslatable; footprints
abound. I understand: you're at a clothes rack at Saks
lifting a white linen blouse at tear's edge wondering.

Fever

Had I possessed the poise to kick
aside my faraway thirst for mornings or the wide
solo in a listening glass emptied of speech, had I
possessed the incorruptible sermons
of windowpanes, or danced a little more in the lush
inscriptions of your gaze—I, who believe in the fauna
of dreams, in the hand that tunes a guitar, in the will
of pages, might have journeyed to you
like ash and abandoned all my fires, and named the epic
light over your shoulders and seized your tumbledown.

Observe His Face

But then when my cell chimed across from
Winthrop Square—yes, it returns like a dead leaf—
from the bench where April wept hopelessly
the day before, as though spring had not arrived bleeding
its greenhouse, or maybe *because* it seeded escape
from her blessed somberness, where the noontime banjoist
with his stompbox played "Bury Me Beneath," where my old
friend Santos, I haven't seen in years, greeted then saw
my panicked face and backed away, for the news
arrived a mistress phoned and me begging forgiveness.

Homecoming

I returned from the Grand Resort
of Solemnity & Sorrow. I drank
my fatigue from a flask and resembled
the man who pointed to his death
in the navel of his son's left eye.
It drilled clear through my skull: boundless
ruin of a pebbly head long decayed
brought forth in a dish. Its sorrow
was vast and soaked the rooms. I go back
to my car. A quite different love disturbs.

Lorca in Eden

Squat by a roadside near Eden, prairie flowers,
barnyard decay, spray of stars bulleting above,
I summon the great poet & pitch my loneliness
across his lake, my chest exploding like milkweed,
nothing more than a stripped hull of seed fluff:
un paisaje prodigioso, pero de una melancolía
infinita . . . No cesa de llover. This moonlight is gruesome,
so many hearts teased to a nakedness then bleached,
frayed, deflated, flapping like scarves in nightwinds—
their radiant mangling all over this meadow of silk.

Myth

I was born scarcely before autumn full of night songs—
my screaming body a codex
of hurting. I tried to name first stars
and bird shadows, prophecy of a greater tempest.
Later it was me supplying earth
her graves, leaves dying in a rainbow
of blossom, spiraling cadavers. On the playground
the last seasonal light firing over slides
and swing sets, those lost notes swirled
and lit my darkened throat.

An Empire of
Hand-Holding &
Park Benches

Autumn Landscape

Seeking what I could not name, my vespertine
spirit loitered evenings down leaf-lined
streets. Stray dogs for company, curbs were empty.
Afar dim poles resembled women. The wind pushed me
like an open hand. Flesh frothed in my head.
I reached for stirred shadows in windows aimed for bed.
When did I not strain for touch? I've a mind
to eat as many stars and refract their dark expanse.
My sadness brings tears, so many victims.
Close your eyes. Here comes the nightmare.

My Awe Is a Weakness

I stood before the TV like a wall of stone.
My network of nerves blacked out.
I should have been chiseling a garden.
I should have chartered a new thought
for a far-off reader imprisoned in his future suburbia.
The evening sky flashed its high definition.
All was night-goggle green, even later her eyes,
which made us aliens unto each other,
and when we went to touch one another as before
like stained glass, nothing flared in us, nothing.

Headstones

Nightfall arrives through hemlocks, etching
tablets of planted bones. Sometimes I hear
my unnamed dead, falsetto beneath wind,
slow whine in the hearth returned to tell me
of absence and loss. I want you naked in a field.
No one is alone. I resent earth, black spirits arrayed
like a shooting gallery. Let's lie in ground mist
unconvinced of farewells. I want never the end plots
of ministers & film reels, commandments whose doors
angle like fallen shadows. Sometimes, leave your face.

Immanence

My own jury I acquitted my inner savage,
known for one-kneed vows to décolletage.
I was aiming for shadows bones make,
namely, the jolt of leaves and roses. A clock struck
and returned the slick smell of snow
on chanterelles. I settled into a naked meadow.
Beneath my right palm disappearing, I brought
an even finer thirst for soil and amateur brawls.
When I faced Nature, I had not a tincture of will.
I tossed her on my bed and did not keep still.

Recondite

The doorknob is consigned. The past survives
our chisel. When he adjourns, he falls back.
The empty bowl feels barely subdued, and doubts
and judges all kiwis. Flightless, small, and somber,
his nails curve like neighboring shorelines.
He thinks how else might he conjure heavens?
He fuels his thirst for naked backs and painted lips.
He connects with nothing. One imagines him
picking scars in the river. He has God's
whorled ears. The summer is all used up.

Prayer

Let me live in the luxury of my friends
like the neatly folded shirt of a carry-on.
Look what we've done to the bees, they say.
Terrorists of silence. They return to the place
of battle and aim their Showguns.
Their handwriting detonates in libraries.
They torture the hairless ears of lieutenants.
O my allies and their valiant songs.
I huddle silent and insatiable
like a spider in a corner of their study.

On the Manner of
Addressing Shadows

that were not ours though we understood their lives,

their sudden advent, daylight painting our façades

when we turned onto Broad Street, oncoming traffic

of strangers, their sudden jolt upright and undulation

should any delivery truck maneuver across their somber torsos

spilling off the curb, even then, still their dark

addiction to our soles. Gloomy sidekicks,

you are cemetery dirt cast unto a cloud that falls

into a city of inevitable demise. You make lords of us,

though we understand your need to detach & walk away.

Overwrought Power Ballad

Over a bed's edge, we were blown away,
a concentric eyewall: my indestructible hunger,
your flowers, gowns, and cake—their own dissolution.
Lightening over our shoulders, the lamps, a black
linen blouse. "To die! To die!" shouted
the marvelous girls, "To die!" In a sacred grove,
we leave nightmares on each other's skin.
I've front row seats to your mumbling sleep.
Let me caw your name; the ground here is
broken. We were late arriving.

Narcissus

Some years ago I recall someone paid attention,
like when an invalid half rises, gripping an armchair—
the street captains and priests busy clicking latches.
The homeless withdrew their luxuries. At night,
distant highways whispered long sighs to the world.

How many hours have I spent crushing mangrove leaves,
turning my face to the unbearable grandeur of this
    heat-soaked
sky? When I spun around, I felt filled with birds.
Still, I returned, wallowing in the brothels of myself.
I thought of my life, caressing more ruins.

Lying

Such a dislike for transparence, he'd overdid
himself, monitoring his stream of shadows. True enough,
he wanted a row of filaments inside like Times Square.
The sockets were dead. To live freely
presages danger in a democracy: major irony.
Such a gift he possessed of reading facial bones,
even in the dark. Hearts placed in a dream
over his city, each encounter an exercise in touch-ups.
In every house, portraits abound. Last night,
he fell asleep listening to sad people sing.

The Giant Swing Ending in a Split

Why was I ashamed to be seen on the waterfront
with her? We both felt the past slip
from our shoulders, rose lipped and listening to
jet engines Doppler across the night.
Wasn't I also me when I lay with her?
Maybe frighteningly more. My sleepsmile
and low whispers hers, too. O
delicious agony, I'm divided right
to my body's historic wharf. I only trust the sweat
salting down my back her fingernail tracks.

Treat the Flame

As if the whole inferno. It's a melodrama
for any gambler embroidered with bells
on her vest who knows if you over-attention
your syntax, every surface is fustian at best.
The sound played is of many foghorns.
All the time I had been dreaming of lost prisms,
the hand's plumage and drift. This is one reason,
I think perhaps I drowned in so many puddles
posing as rivers, the eloquence of mirrors.
You are right to detest your inner pyro.

Periplum

The notion that the land gave us flying
you said, or, conceivably, flying made us
aware of the notion of land was your most recent
attempt to strike a lasting chord. Of course,
this exposed our admiration for the hard-hatted surveyor
wide-eyeing a dumpy level. There is in me someone
who would rather fall out a window, Buster Keaton–like,
and come up important like a tripod. Gurdjieff nearly
cried for collaboration. We both pointed to his
eminently readable mustache: graspable yet airborne.

My Face in the ATM Screen

O the camera that lies in wait
like a mugger behind the glass.
So very toothsome, I mistook for
a zealot. My funds were secure but not me,
for I was lovesick. Rewind the surveillance.
Observe my face. I am unhappy
despite the approaching spit of bills
flapping near my zipper. A single day
of concatenated cams streaming reveals
it is my hour to bottle the monarchs.

Maithuna

What were we reaching for, pouring
the storm of our days those first few hours
into each others' mouths? And what sadnesses
were we abandoning? What wars were we
marching against? And just how many hearts
you asked were stolen and how many rightfully
mine? How did I come to imagine building
a city of flowerboxes? Or hear your people
whispering in between the planting? And then,
when in the next few hours did we cease?

Here the Sea

Her eyes have made a drifter of me,
this, the first day of winter. Is it natural
the future resembles lime grapes? What cost
will I pay for the grief of a solarium?
I wouldn't have thought I'd fall so easily for
bejeweled eddies. I am seduced by the warmth
coming off her eyelids. My mailbox is oblivious
to my new breathing. As they say in Petra,
I like you here inside a mountain.
She came toward me through her smile.

Brash and Ambitious

The glances tumbling wide: foggy fields
of purple vetch when I lift their faces to me
in the rounded bowl of a wineglass.
I ponder other worries: recipes of failure:
the matchless kiss turned affectionate.
Once, as my hand guided a woman's lower back
to a camp, an inscrutable fox followed
then led, crossing a moonlit path up a knoll.
Discussing de Sade by a plate of gouda, one laughed,
I want ravishment, complete ravishment.

Leave It All Up to Me

All we want is to succumb to a single kiss
that will contain us like a marathon
with no finish line, and if so, that we land
like newspapers before sunrise, halcyon
mornings like blue martinis. I am learning
the steps to a foreign song: her mind
was torpedo, and her body was storm,
a kind of *Wow*. All we want is a metropolis
of Sundays, an empire of hand-holding
and park benches. She says, "Leave it all up to me."

Zucchini

Since that first kiss in the lobby on Boerum Hill, I've fallen
in love with Brooklyn, and the risky ledges of subway
platforms, and the way a small letter of light emerges
out of darkness to whisk me away, if I want, to the island
of bankers and foodies. But I prefer the smoked prosciutto,
and the carpaccio, and the branzino at *Vini e Olii's*
where François and Catherine kiss both cheeks,
and a whole village of monarchs flickers in my knees.

What comes to us is the pure speed of our hands pressed
through the years, and occasionally, scrambled eggs at
    midnight,
when I tumble into her full-throated eyes, which do not
    apologize
for learning to sing as men fell from her skies like popped
    balloons.

Forecast

Whichever way our shoulders move, there's joy.
Make a soft hollow noise. We've our own hourglass
and no one else to blame. I thought of our lives,
caressing ruins through half-opened windows.
I hear our prayers rising. I sing to you, now,
like scented candles, your ferocious wolf.
I no longer want this weather on my breath
or the many recognizable texts of our celestial holes.
A ceiling fan turns above. The arson is in us.
This is the year I'll contemplate the fire-fangled sky.

Notes

"Going to Meet the Man" and "Headstones" were inspired by the visual art of William Cordova and commissioned by the University of Vermont Fleming Museum for its exhibition More than Bilingual: William Cordova and Major Jackson.

"*Mondes en Collision*" was inspired by the life of Immanuel Velikovsky. In 1950, the catastrophist Velikovsky authored the controversial book *Worlds in Collision*, which radically hypothesized that in earlier times an electromagnetic disorder of the solar system caused Venus and Mars to closely approach the Earth, thus disturbing its rotation. He postulated these close contacts with other planets made credible events humans normally discredit as mythology or unproven biblical stories such as the Exodus. Despite the popularity of the book, he suffered great hostilities from the academic and scientific communities who all but ignored him, which, ironically, only increased his demand on the lecture circuit. He died on November 17, 1979, in Princeton, New Jersey.

"After Riefenstahl" alludes to German director and producer Berta Helene Amalie Riefenstahl, better known as Leni Riefenstahl, who in 1935 made the film *Triumph of the Will*, which documented the 1934 convention of the Nazi Party at Nürnberg and scarily dramatized the power and pageantry of the Nazi movement. She has been hailed as one of "the most technically talented Western filmmakers of her era." I take creative liberties with scholars' hypothesis of her romantic interest in Adolf Hitler.

The full quote I excerpt in "Roof of the World" is taken from "Existentialism Is a Humanism," a famous lecture by John Paul Sartre, and reads as follows: "We are left alone, without excuse. That is what I mean when I say that man is condemned to be free. Condemned, because he did not create himself, yet is nevertheless at liberty, and from the moment that he is thrown into this world he is responsible for everything he does."

In his translator's note to Thucydides's *History of the Peloponnesian War*, Rex Warner states, "Even Plato would be easier," which sparked the poem "Said the Translator."

"Jane Says" is in homage to Perry Farrell, lead singer of the famed rock band Jane's Addiction, and his ex-housemate Jane Bainter, a former heroin addict who served as inspiration to the group's most famous song "Jane Says."

"You, who carry daylight on your face" scantily borrows phrases from Saint Augustine's *Confessions*.

Dante Gabriel Rossetti's poem "Last Visit to the Louvre," a short ekphrastic poem in response to the paintings of Peter Paul Rubens and Antonio Allegri da Correggio, inspired "Poem Beginning with a Line by Dante Rossetti."

"Thinking of Lucretius" ponders briefly, specifically at the title, Latin poet Titus Lucretius Carus, who authored the epic poem *On the Nature of Things*, which makes clear Epicurus and his ethical philosophy of hedonism and devotion to the pursuit of sensuous pleasures.

The poem "Delicious. I love you. Goodbye." takes its title from a line in John Ashbery's poem "Withered Compliments," which can be found in his book *Hotel Lautréamont*.

"Lorca in Eden" quotes Federico García Lorca's letter to his friend

Angel del Rio about his ten days in Eden, Vermont, in the summer of August 1929, which translates to: "A wonderful landscape but an infinite melancholy. It is constantly raining."

"My Awe Is a Weakness" takes its cue from the United States' military doctrine of rapid, overwhelming dominant power, "Shock and Awe." On March 20, 2003, the United States led an invasion into the country of Iraq, allegedly "to disarm Iraq of weapons of mass destruction (WMD), to end Saddam Hussein's support for terrorism, and to free the Iraqi people." Military officials described their strategy as one of "shock and awe."

"Periplum" cites the Greco-Armenian mystic and philosopher Georgii Ivanovich Gurdjieff, who basically asserted that we live our lives as though we are sleeping and that we must transcend this sleeping state by achieving great vitality and awareness. He titled his program of self-development "The Fourth Way."

About the Author

Major Jackson is the author of three collections of poetry: *Holding Company* (Norton, 2010), *Hoops* (Norton, 2006), and *Leaving Saturn* (University of Georgia, 2002), winner of the Cave Canem Poetry Prize and finalist for a National Book Critics Circle Award. *Hoops* was a finalist for an NAACP Image Award in the category of Outstanding Literature—Poetry. He is a recipient of a Whiting Writers' Award and has been honored by the Pew Fellowship in the Arts and the Witter Bynner Foundation in conjunction with the Library of Congress. He served as a creative arts fellow at the Radcliffe Institute for Advanced Study at Harvard University and as the Jack Kerouac Writer-in-Residence at the University of Massachusetts–Lowell. Currently, he is the Sidney Harman Writer-in-Residence at Baruch College. He has guest lectured and taught at many institutions including Columbia University, New York University, and Xavier University of New Orleans. Major Jackson is the Richard Dennis Green and Gold Professor at University of Vermont and a core faculty member of the Bennington Writing Seminars. He serves as the poetry editor of the *Harvard Review*.